REAL DEPICTIONS OF YOUR MIRROR LIFE

TO KNOW YOURSELF

CHESH SPIRE

Copyright © Chesh Spire
All Rights Reserved.

This book has been published with all efforts taken to make the material error-free after the consent of the author. However, the author and the publisher do not assume and hereby disclaim any liability to any party for any loss, damage, or disruption caused by errors or omissions, whether such errors or omissions result from negligence, accident, or any other cause.

While every effort has been made to avoid any mistake or omission, this publication is being sold on the condition and understanding that neither the author nor the publishers or printers would be liable in any manner to any person by reason of any mistake or omission in this publication or for any action taken or omitted to be taken or advice rendered or accepted on the basis of this work. For any defect in printing or binding the publishers will be liable only to replace the defective copy by another copy of this work then available.

TO

My mom, dad , cousines and siblings

and to them who supported me...

Contents

Foreword — *vii*

Preface — *ix*

Acknowledgements — *xi*

Prologue — *xiii*

Author's Note — *xv*

PART-1

1. Your Life — 3

2. Things Of Life — 8

3. Way — 9

4. Bounded Unbondings — 12

5. One From One — 14

6. What Makes You — 16

7. The Aspirations — 18

8. Accordance Of Envision — 21

9. Ways Of World — 23

10. The Resolution — 25

11. Bigger Ways Doesn't Mean — 27

12. Ways Are Waves — 30

13. Experience — 32

14. Persisting Perseverance — 34

PART-2

15. Things To Yourself — 39

16. Doesn't Change Always — 41

17. Wonders & Mirror — 42

Contents

18. Things In Life 44

THING TO KNOW

19. Aspirations &way 49

20. Weird 51

21. Curioisity 53

22. Depictions Of Life 54

23. Life Is On Everything 56

24. Know 58

25. Verse 59

Index 61

Other Works From Author 65

Upcoming 67

About Author 69

Right Of First Publication 71

Notes 73

About You 75

FOREWORD

One is prime mover of his life, there will be many choices in life but one should choose the perfect one which makes him to know about it and makes him to reach another... And there is a primary thing in our life is to know ourselves and lives.

Preface

We have a beautiful life and which is a reflector of our thoughts. This book is about you and your life, to make you aware of yourself and your abilities. This book is not about one and it absolutely about everyone to make them know about their lives and to make them to persist in the world. The present humans who are living are forgotten about their lives completely and working in the world which they is being called developing world and modern world. But knowing and realizing their actual life and their original selves is a way in which people might discover way that will make them to be without sadness. The main cause for the things that make you sad is the things that you are not interested in and being done by forcing yourself or by the spotlight of world. And you should know about you and your aspirations as well as dreams. You can't always say yes to the world and you can't always do the things in a forcible way to you .when you realize the day then your world will be the best thing to make the life in better way. The day of realization could be in soon....

You are in the world of wise where world might make you to fall into trap but don't bound yourself to the trap. There are many things you can do but world could say you can't but actually there is nothing to search in a thing than a little interest and the happiness. And you should do things in a serious way where you can addicted to it do it in a way that makes you feel better. You are the absolute one in the world to change it. Know yourself I a way that you life can be realized and make you to reach your own aspirations. Do not do anything in a painful way where you could be hurt do it in a way where it heals you. Don't be afraid of world and future because you can change your life with the thoughts. There are millions of way but don't be bounded to the one. Get into the millions if it is possible and never stop getting into them. This book is about you and your life, to make you to know about you and your abilities.

Acknowledgements

This book is written based not only on my experience but also on what I have witnessed throughout the years. To finish this work it had taken many weeks and months. Everyone who was around me helped tremendously to finish this work. I thank everyone who helped and supported me and also the ones who gave ideas for improving my skills. This might be helpful for some people who feel differently about themselves. I think by completing this book I learned many things and pushed myself through many things. I hope by reading this you would learn something and know something.

This book is a description of the philosophy of man. It describes a modern human's daily life and what he does in his daily life. I think this book is different because it does not just contain quotations, poems, or stories of people who have gone through life's trials and tribulations. There is always a lesson to be learned in everything we do in life, no matter how small or how large it may seem. As a result of this learning, we are able to move from being a neophyte to a veteran. This has resulted in me writing about what we make as a result of our experiences.

I mentioned this book title as "Real depictions of your mirror life" because pictures that describe events are called depictions and I wanted to describe human life as a view of pictures. And life is a mirror which reflects and the life on the other side of the mirror is called mirror life. The purpose of this book is to help humans get to know themselves better.

PROLOGUE

"When you find yourself in the world that makes you, you will realize the real or the true one of you"

--chesh spire

Author's Note

From chesh spire...

Everybody is a beginner and neophyte in instinct, everything is new to a beginner, in our lives we go from stage of neophyte to stage of vetaran and it takes much time or our entire time in life to acquire and complete this process. in spite of this we must be known that we were not machines or other, when we were in stage of the neophyte we be afraid to do everything in first but we will be able acquire the experience and we move to the things that we afraid of at some moments.

in spite being in loop of aged life we can actually make lives to know more thing as like learning about the life before the life ends or at the end. i would say everyone must get an knowledge about the life and everyone should know what they were doing in their lives. as we get older we get closer to the stage of vetaran and we become experts in making things or in learning and this is where all things startup to make to forget about our actual life, we get involved into the work and we spend more time to the work. we won't be able to get out of this. the best is to know the way and rid off these bounding from the life. we must know the ways to be happy and know the ways that makes us sad. we must acquire the experince that to lead life in good way. we must know somethings which are important to ourselves in straight in some time. We will spend our most of the time in working and we sometimes forget our important things in life, however our work in world is for needs for living an artificial life but our work in life is for survivial like a true human who knew about his responsibilites.

PART-1

CHOOSING WAYS AND KNOWING ABILITIES

KNOW THE ACTUAL ACCORDANCE OF THINGS AND DETERMINATIONS

No matter what world is in but follow your actual one

I

YOUR LIFE

You have to make yourself to reach a different ways and you have to make your life in a unique way where you will experience and show others how to choose the ways. The most things people say about their life is to reach things but it isn't for it . It was for the things, dreams and aspirations and to know the expereince of the aspirations and dreams. World is not an actual opponent but world isn't a actual supporter to. Many people might be right in their way but they are not in the way of happiness. things can make you happy and they can even make your sad and you should not make your happiness get fallen for the things always. If you persist your life in a way where you change it like waves in the ocean. You could be the one to make your life and make it to reach it in a particular way. You are one to lead you life and you are the one to create the ways to reach your aspirations.

Many people in world might think that they were reaching the thing but they were actually wrong if you look deep in the way then you can look into the deep to the aspiration which way wanted to accord you. You no need go into the aspirations because they lead the confusion and you can raise the questions in your mind such as the purpose and the reason for the aspirators. As we talk about the reason for the aspirations we would the main thing is survival the one who just need survival can survive anywhere but the one who wants to live only in particular place wanted to develop his abilities it can be stated that if want just survival the world is place and you need some dominance they you get a specific place where you think you are only one but if fact there will be millions. You doesn't have to go on the particular way what other and the crowd in your diversity may choose but you need to go on the way you are interested in alike if you like to go with the painting then you just go and don't think life is only for the particular thing it is for everything it was in your own hands in understanding about the life and understanding about yourself and about your life. You can get an uncountable aspirations and don't think you can't all of them in real you can actually do everything you wanted to do in life because it is in your own hands.

It could be difficult to hear and tell you that you been bounding to the way in which nothing different happens.Your life is an amazing gift to handle and to you are the prime mover to your life who can lead you. The present how long you hide yourself from the world it long the world wanted to know. You just can't hide yourself and your true one can come out one day and show the world his ability. You are the one in the world who can change it but it just admires as changed and it doesn't change always. World is the weird thing in our lives which is a composed of illusions and was always to distract you. The one who doesn't choose the world could be the one fallen in words of world but he always reaches the efficient and he be as the pioneer of many things. It doesn't always depend on the world whether you are capable or not. There is not limit that everybody should be known in everything. The specified person will have their certain specific ability and he made himself for it and if he doesn't let the world to choose his ability then he can be the true one in the world of opposes. Everything that world wants you to do can be for you but it wasn't the thing that was you are interested and specified in.

The saw many people who always wanted to get rid of the world ways but they made them to be only the choice. It does happen when are the one who has ability to do but you cannot express it to the particular. Don't let anything in your way to stop you from there. When you are determined then you could be the one who can reach the way of aspirations and you could be the one who can reach the way of new thing.

"you have a great ability and know it, reach it , modify it and don't let it go out of your life."

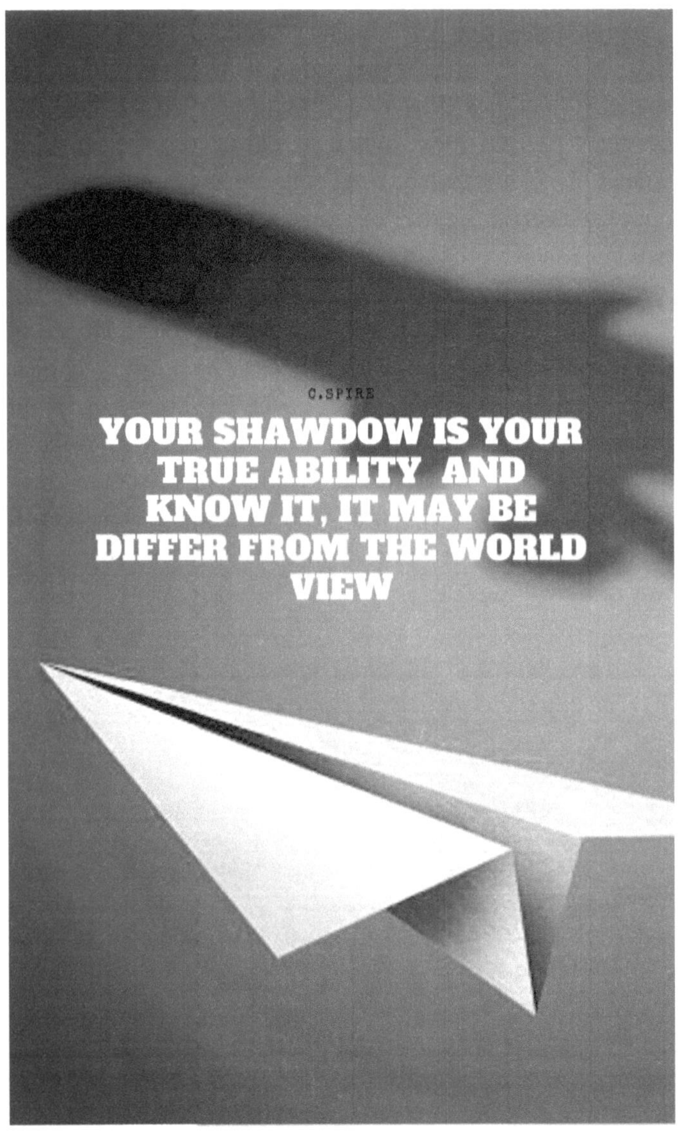
C.SPIRE
YOUR SHAWDOW IS YOUR
TRUE ABILITY AND
KNOW IT, IT MAY BE
DIFFER FROM THE WORLD
VIEW

The real one

Know you true ability, it can differ from world's view

II
THINGS OF LIFE

Things in the life are unavoidable they come off and they go off but it depends on the particular mind on how he is going to take. In a one's life he can create and lead many things. But I wonder how these things are created from one. Things create from thoughts the thoughts which they wanted to be in different way and the thoughts will create the aspirations and they lead to the creation of the things. In our lives we can do everything in a different which could lead us to the innovation of a new one. We think, we speak and we do everything and our lives are not bounded to anything it's our lives to live one till the particular time. We doesn't have a particular thing to reach we doesn't have a particular work to do. We are here to design ourselves and we are here to be ourselves and we are the ones to lead us. Never forget to be yourself in the world even when the world opposes. we are not just giving importance to machines and we are with the machines like a machine.

III
WAY

The way you choose to achieve a specific thing could be the best or weird. The best way you choose doesn't mean to the way that leads to specific. But the weird way you choose could make you to reach an undiscovered thing in your life. The undiscovered thing in your life could be the thing that makes your life. What does exactly the undiscovered thing mean to you? The undiscovered thing is in the repulsive way to your exact way. The way could be weird not to you and for the world but if you persist then you are the pioneer to the specific thing. When you are persisting in the way and determined to persist till long you could face the difficulties in the things to achieve then you can make the thing to be revealed to world.

When you realize that you can't persist in the same way you choose then your life could get in the persisting way. The persisting way is the new and exact way that they lead you to the unspecified. Reaching a specified way with the way could be harder than reaching an unspecified way with defined way. When you find the way that only leads you to the life, try whether it is or not the only one. Try the way which you think that leads your life. But there is no specific way that makes your life. There are only the subways that make you to reach your dreams. Try a way or an unknown process that they can make you to reach an unspecified progress.

It doesn't about the choosing a way it about you and to make you by yourself to try the weird thing and new things to get your life be happy.

WAY ARE UNREMMITING

Perisist on your way

IV
BOUNDED UNBONDINGS

Spirit of proving themselves doesn't depend on the way you're travelling which it depends on the way of persistence you are reaching in the way of perseverance and

Find youself in the world which you are trying to hide. Find you to make your life to persist in a way. You can hide you. Because the things you make and thoughts you imagine leads you into the way of fantasy. Fantasy is way leads to aspirations of your life. Find you in the way to modify with thoughts. Every person in the universe has the spirit and aspiration to prove them. But the thing is the world doesn't accord you the way that leads you to you. The spirit that you get from life is more effective than you get from world.

Life is not same always. Life is a mysterious thing that was everything. Your memories and you are the part of it. The farther you reach the farther you make. Life can be changed with your thoughts.

Things changes with thoughts. Thoughts creates from imagination. When the world doesn't change the life makes a way which accords you the experience of different world. Unremitting life of the unremitting thoughts leads to way of perseverance.

Knots in one's life are common but unbounding them is a contradiction

V
ONE FROM ONE

World makes the ways for people but some people makes the ways for world. Those are the one of all time with the spirit of ways. They can lead the world. They persists with the time their spirit and make another one. World doesn't makes anything till the drops of work shed on the sea. Way of pertinacity lead by way of persistence till you reaches the way of remitting. you are most efficient one in the world cause you can choose your thoughts and your life to be persisted.

One from one

VI
WHAT MAKES YOU

The one thing in life that always makes you be good is you happiness. But have you ever wondered the how the happiness comes to your life. First thing that comes in your mind can be a word like reaching the dream or any other thing that you like. But it is different from the daily happiness that makes you is work. The most of people spend their time on their works but the works they does really accord them happiness. May be not but some people who work for their happiness are and for all sake are the great ones in the planet. Because the work they do could be fun or could be easy or they has more interest on that. The real meaning of reaching a dream is the result that makes you higher than your actual place. But know that your life always cannot be made by the same things. The happiness in your life doesn't always come from the things or work you do for living. But it comes from your mind and your heart when you are truly interested. Happiness is the most precious thing that everyone has and do not get it spoiled. Don't destroy you experience with the things and work you do. When you realize that your life doesn't have a specific thing to reach always then you could be in the world of experience.

The life you are living in is bounded with the experience to move on with other things behind you do. Cause being a human we have a particular thing to reach always. When you want you reach something then know in which way you are going. Your thoughts in your life create the opportunities to you to make you on the way.

We made ourselves to be

VII
THE ASPIRATIONS

Accordance of optimism in the way of life doesn't come always from things it comes from the aspirations and dreams in accordance to do them. Aspirations are unremitting dreams that one is willing to do, they accord optimism to reach the things and experience to make the ways, things doesn't makes and accords you ways or specific things. Always do the works with optimism and reach the aspirations with it. The best way to reach a specific thing is to think in the positive manner of reaching it.

You could get many difficulties in reaching the specific but they are just obstructers to the ways and never bother about the things that distract you. Make the ways and build your own things to get you aspired thing. Aspirations are the persisting things of one's dreams and they are innovators to the world. The aspirations arise from the fantasy of one's dreams. The humans are gifted with the great power called imagination which they make everything and lead the one thought to aspiration and makes the one to reach. Life is a mirror which reflections your thoughts and you, you cannot hide from it because you need to persist. The most specified thing in the ones is from one life. remember you may work hours a day, days a week and years but you may earn or you may still work but happiness and the aspirations to learning things doesn't be provide by the work. You should lead your life in the way which makes you learn and ends with amelioration.

Don't just think

VIII

ACCORDANCE OF ENVISION

"The world accords you the envision of your ability but you must persist and choose behind it"

World is the weird and it can make one person to rise or fall and it can accord the subways to the way that lead you to the dreams or your aspirations but world may accord you the way that leads or reach you to exact or even some lesser but you must choose or get in to the way which reaches you beyond the way to ameliorate your experience and to makes your aspirations and dreams and to know the things. World is biggest illusion which creates some opponents and it also solves them some times. You can choose your way because you are the prime mover of your life and you are persisting one in the world of rush. Everything in the world is created from ones thoughts and aspirations when they reach they may not be stopped because the curiosity of the man is the world best and powerful thing which can create wonders and makes some to reach their unknown dreams and aspiration without making it as aspiration. Envision In the world could be best if you imagine the best because it was the assuming and which may leads you to the thoughts and assumption of the future things. Envision can be changed when a person is always on the way of curiosity and is determined to persist in the way of curiosity.

IX
WAYS OF WORLD

"World can provided you many ways but choose a way that is prominent to the existing one for a persisting dream"

They are many way you could choose with the experience but the prominent one always leads to the prominent dreams and the prominent dreams leads to the pursuance of experience for your mirror life. The most effective way to get into way is to think about the thing. When you get into to the way, you should persist than going back. Know the things that make you to choose the way.

Your way can be opposite to the world ways

X

THE RESOLUTION

Know the things that you wanted to do and you don't, replace the unwanted things with the new ones to make yourself to know about new things. Things you meet in life are unremitting and you can learn about them if you wanted to. Get in the way of different aspiration and which can be aspired by the different thoughts. Go into the fantasy to your aspirations and know your life in the particular way. Your fantasy doesn't have an end and you can imagine anything anytime nothing stops you and it and be and know what you truly know and create. You can create wonders with thoughts and you can discover the most beautiful natures of world. All the thoughts are the wonders to get. Thoughts make us to be innovative and to be an explorer. Make a resolution to yourself to find you in your ways and you happiness which was actually led by the thoughts. You could be in any position but realize about you in the efficient way that you're best to be in the world which makes you to learn even when you had fallen.

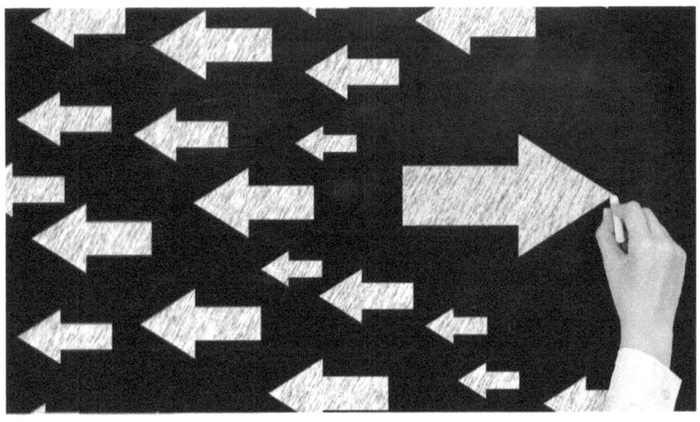

Make resolution to yourself

XI

BIGGER WAYS DOESN'T MEAN

When you choose the bigger way and you might think that they could make you to reach bigger things in life but actually they can't mean to be as they were. All the ways I life could make you to reach somewhere but the bigger way does the same thing. And the ways which are different form normal ones can make you to reach bigger thing. All things in life can't be only reached through the ways but they can't be created in your life through your experience and you thinking. Bigger in life are same as the smaller ones.

WAYS DOESN'T MEAN

CHESH SPIRE

XII

WAYS ARE WAVES

"*Ways are waves they don't make rich they make
you reach to the things you made*"

The world has many ways they are similar to the waves which leads unknown experiencing thing. As the waves leads you to the unknown places when you stuck in ocean. As you realize that every way is wave that accords you experience to overcome a sea. You can acquire experience by travelling in different ways. Everything in world plays a crucial role when you realize they are.

Ways are waves

XIII
EXPERIENCE

Experience that you acquire from the things you made leads the things you can make. Experience that world accords you to make you reach the way that world extends and makes the ways shorter. The experience that you acquire accords you the ways that leads to ways to reach your aspirations. Experience you acquired from the world is not persistent than you acquire from your life. Nothing is persistent than your thoughts. World can accord you experience of pessimism or optimism. Its depends on you that how you going to acquire the experience

Make yourself with your experience

XIV

PERSISTING PERSEVERANCE

"Perseverance accords you the way to reach persistence makes your aspirations to things"

Perseverance leads you to the way that accords you experience of persistence. Makes you to rise even you fallen in world. Persistence makes you to continue in the way to reach you aspiration before the ways ends. Persistence in life makes you reach the thoughts to works to things. Life is a persisting thing that never stops but it cans makes you stop. Nothing in life is persistent than your perseverance.

You may have a particular choice but they were not persistence to the whole life. Your life has many great choices but they will come till the end of your life the thing and thoughts can be changed. And don't be on the same way till you reach the end of the way and you get into the things where you reached. There will many choices and ways in life however world may think you be chosen the particular one but it could be different from the things you wanted to reach.

Persistence in mind can't make way to disappear

PART-2

WORLD AND YOU

XV
THINGS TO YOURSELF

Never hide yourself in the world cause it can be known as it was hidden.

Never hide you in yourself. It doesn't hide you from sight of world and from sight of yourself. Your life reveals you as your thoughts are in your imagination. Imagine a life in a better way with evacuating thoughts can't make yourself as you think. You can't give it up and you can't take it up. Reveal yourself to the world to evacuate pessimism from you and your life.

Never leave something before you start it. Never give up to yourself. Accepting failure in life gives you optimism to push on your life with new thoughts and with a weird experience. Accepting your failure before you try gives you pessimism to can't take your life to dream. Reached to the mid journey and revealing to give up it doesn't push you on your life. It can make you fall from the world you designed and modifying with thoughts.

Never let your way to push you on pessimism. Never blame yourself and others in your life. It makes you to create you pessimism in your life. The thoughts never leave you until you reveal them to yourself. Blaming others doesn't leave you from your thoughts it pulls you into the way with pessimism. Find the way to stop your life to travel on the way of pessimism. Choose a perfect way that ends with amelioration.

XVI

DOESN'T CHANGE ALWAYS

"World doesn't change it creates an illusion to you which it changed know the truth beyond the illusion to persist your life."

The world doesn't change always as you want to be. It can makes rise and can makes you fall it was unknown to everyone. It can make as best even as a least. But never stop with that result. It depends on you how you going change your life. The world makes you reach till mid journey of your life. It shows a sub way to find your new way at end of every journey. It can make your envision as you take it. It can end with optimism or pessimism. But remember it was not persistent to your life.Nothing in world are persistent except your thoughts. Make your life as you can with the thoughts of your life.

XVII
WONDERS & MIRROR

Wonders are with you . They may change your way even you life. Thoughts are wonders in your life but wonders can happen after a try. Your thought has ability to create or destroy anything. Thoughts have ability to change the world in few seconds. They make you high as you reach with them. They are wonders.Everything in world has a verge except your thought.

A mirror always reflects you and your thoughts to your world. Life is a mirror to yourself it reflects the thoughts that you imagine. A mirror is always in front of you to reflect your thought and reveals you to the world. You can't hide from the mirror. It reveals you to the world to create your world as you imagine.

"The world is innovative with the thoughts created in fantasy of people, the world without fantasy is the world without innovative. Fantasy is the way that

leads to aspirations of your life."

The world can't persist without the thoughts of people who makes world brighter than it emits. Fantasy can turn a world into scintillating star. It can make you to the verges of world makes reach your thoughts and emits you into way leads to aspirations and hopes.

know your life and abilities

XVIII
THINGS IN LIFE

"The world can make you fall and even it can rise you up but never stop with that world accords you"

Every living thing on earth has fallen once in life to rise them up. They can rise with their experience or with pessimism.The world makes you fall and fall from every step you build but growing pessimism in you makes you fall directly from the floors to ground. The world that traps you in world and makes you fall forever and builds pessimism in you.You can make you rise as you fall. Rise from the world before you fall.

You can fight back to your fall and your fear to raise high as you can. Your life is like a ocean with the great dangers. There is only a way to escape is the cliff on the land. Your dreams are in top of cliff. There is way to reach is climb up to reach your dreams. But you fall as the high you reach from the world. But every time you fall gives you new experience every time you rise gives yourself a new way to reach your dreams.

You can rise yourself with the help of the ways and experiences accorded by the world. Develop optimism in you to avoid pessimism and to persist your life to make you rise from the fallen world. Your thoughts are always wonders. They can help you to rise you from the world. Your imagination is the main source of innovation in the world. It can make you try weird things and gives you weird conclusions. Weird experiences accord you the key of way to make you rise from the fallen world.

Rising optimism in you gives you the best way to reach your dreams. It is a hidden inner power that makes rise even you are at bottom. Your life without optimism is a world without having its innovation. Rise the inner power in you. Imagine best envision in your life and make your life to persist on way which reaches your dreams. Your life is mysterious riddle to yourself. It takes much time and much effort to solve it.You can rise the optimism in you by withdrawing pessimism from yourself. Make yourself reach the weird thing to get weird experiences. Make yourself as a resistant to the way that makes you fall. Choose a perfect way that ends with amelioration and the way that leads dreams. Never choose a way that makes you fall and make yourself as resistant to the way which makes you fall from your dreams. Make yourself to go on the way that reaches your dreams.How do you make yourself as a resistant to the way that makes you fall.Make yourself resistant by using you experience when you have fallen last time. Experiences gives you the confidence that you are organized for the way and you can even rise even you fallen. Build optimism in you to resist from the way. Imagining the best makes you to reach the way. It accords the experience of success. It makes you rise quick even you have fallen. Make your way to reach dreams of yourself. Make your way with the thoughts of your life. it can be odd or old but create a way that makes rise.

THING TO KNOW

THERE BE ALWAYS A THING TO LEARN IN THE WORLD

XIX

ASPIRATIONS &WAY

The world has many ways to reach something and it let you into every way to reach something
WAY LEADS TO ASPIRATIONS.Expectations and the hopes are the aspirations leads to the way with optimism to persist your life.Expectations can make you to create a world in your life. Hopes can lead the expectations to persist your life. The world accords you every chance to move your life in your way
PRIME MOVER OF YOUR LIFE

You are the prime mover of your life assist yourself to persist your life. You can make the decisions of your life through imagining a weird thoughts and taking weird decisions. Assist yourself to make your life in perfect shape. The ways in your life can end earlier than they begin. NEVER CHOOSE A WAY WHICH ENDS BEFORE YOU REACH. Never choose a way which ends before you reach. Imagine journey in a way leads to dreams. Imagine a way that ending before you reach to your dreams diverts you into a way with pessimism and makes you fall from world you created. Choose a way that shouldn't be end earlier than you reach. It should assist you to a new way to reach it. Everything in world is distinct and even old but we never stop

it can be odd or old to reach. Your way can be odd or old to reach but choose a way which ends with amelioration. Amelioration accords you a weird experience to make your way serene.

Your way can old. It can be an old process to make but it can be perfect to make. It can be odd to make. Try the odd things to make something odd in your life. Everything in world reveals something to everyone either a riddle or some clues to trace it

world tries to reveal you. World doesn't reveal your trait it reveal a way to reach it. The world doesn't reveal you a direct way to reach your trait. It reveals you a riddle to trace it and reach your trait. The world doesn't reveal a way for anything. It leaves the riddle to trace your subway to reach your way. Envision of yourself is not persistent it is part of your imagination

YOUR TRAIT DOESN'T REVEAL

Your trait doesn't reveal your envision it reveals your way of imagining. You can change your trait but your way of thinking doesn't leave you. It makes you to reach your thoughts it makes you high as you go with it. Your trait can't decide by your envision. It changes by thoughts of your imagination. Envision is fantasy of yourself.

XX

WEIRD

Life is a mysterious thing in world. Life is the mysterious I have seen in this world. It can make anyone rise or fall. Because nothing accords you things without your presence in that thing. They don't make your life. They don't make your way. They just accord you experience. When you fall from your things never give up to yourself. That increases pessimism in you. Make you fall permanently from the world. Time is weirdest thing in world. Time is unstoppable and it was weirdest thing in world making if you are persisting then your past would be worse than present and your future is better than present. If you increasing pessimism then your past is better than present. Your present is better than future. It depends on you which way you are choosing in your life either to persist or to fall.World is weirdest thing in your life.

"World is weird it doesn't change. It has ability to your thoughts"

World is the weirdest thing in the world. This can't be changed. It may change your thoughts into a way of optimism or pessimism. It depends on you how you going to change your life. with the thoughts of your life. Things can make you afraid of them

Things can make you afraid of them. Things in life are mysterious can make fall and rise even make you afraid about them. They can change only with your thought. Never give up to thing you start when they end. Never let something to criticize you in your life. They can't make you fall or rise. **There are no verges** for the dreams to reach them. Dreams in life have no verges to reach them. They make you to terminate you in a loop that ends with a dream by starting another. Your thoughts can make you to stop in the place where you stand cause they you to make you.

XXI
CURIOISITY

A world for the one who thinks other than it was a tiny thing, he don't search for the asked questions but may rather search for the unasked ones in his life, there be a great thing in life that makes to find every secrete is our curiosity. It was a leading source to the innovation and was a undestroyable thing in one's life. curiosity is a best way to make a world innnovative. a curious person has ability to discover and as well as to create. he can be a pioneer. curiosity is bounded with many things that makes a person to improve his way of thinking and it can influence his thoughts. aspirations gets created from thougths and thoughts are directed by curiosity. one can make remarkable changes in the world if he does persist in his true way.

XXII

DEPICTIONS OF LIFE

There is one main depiction in life is ourself. we can be known by some one throught our trait we they cannot know our way of thinking. We are the ones who decide the way of representing our lives. and we are the one who decides the way of life. World creates an illusion as it is changed however in reality it doesn't changes these are the illusions of world and never fell for them. If you want to create or perform a work because of your curiosity in knowledge, you can do it cause the things which develops after being curious makes you to stick to the work. The main thing in this world which actually making people to work is not curiosity or any other related in learning it was actually the malady of altior. Altior malady or altior notion makes one to become the dominant or to become desire in dominance in the particular. And another thing that makes these people is conditional imitation, Which was the counterfeit to yourself. however it was actually a short way or escaping from one's own innovation and imagination. Never follow someone's way blindly or exactly and know where does way of others reach.

we know we can't be forever but we can know the things that lasts forever. our life is just doesn't made to struck in the loop it actually made to know our life and our world. we are the true one in our lives that we must be known as we. as our lives are not made to be forever we should let our parts of life to be in it's way and to be in search of our happiness. Our abilities and thoughts has no edges to get bounded they are the boundaries for many things untill you reaslise.

Make your life on your own

XXIII

LIFE IS ON EVERYTHING

Human life is a bounded with thoughts and the aspirations and the relations in between them but the main thing in life is to get enough happiness and some memories to your life. Fill your blank life with days and make your life to be on the best way and the best things in the life. most of us spend our whole lives living for something that just knowing the ways to know their life.

Peaceful ones don't fight with each other-
But rather with themselves,
Not every moment needed an explanation,
A memory indeed,
not everyday everything would be same,
somethings can be in contrary,
not every step should be towards dreams,
sometimes it can towards in contrary to sadness,
not every wall is a hider nor a barrier,
not everything is harmless nor harmer,

to know everythings we doesn't need skills
indeed of understanding them in time.
One who know about the world
might affect it's direction,
but one who know about his life
can steer himself without the world
(from chapter-1, life of pheonix by c.spire)

XXIV

KNOW

A human must know about himself and one must know about his traits. your traits doesn't reveal anything but they can influence. if you think more philosophically there is nothing that is important or there is thing that is important. a way which is followed by the millions in some day gets closed and another appears. we should find new way which can lead us to the unknown things that makes something better. the better thing to do in this world is not get inspire. it makes us to follow towards the way which is not much new.

XXV

VERSE

A human must be bounded to his responsibilties not of things but of self, one's self boundaries are his steps towards realization of his life and way of living, one's philosophy in entire is simlar to his trait which he developed. One must be in way of good and one must be in the way of life. a mirror can reflect exact thing even it is good or bad. a mirror relfects every deed till it's prime mover overcomes it. a mirror is not just a reference to normal life inspite it is reference to the life of human which is seen by the world. sometimes mirrors evokes ourselves and in some moments we must evoke them to make our envision true.

Reveal yourself to your life to know your envision to create yourself and modify with your imagination and the thoughts created from the imagination.

-chesh spire

Index

index contains spell of word, meaning and part of speech.

- **aspiration** /aspəˈreɪʃ(ə)n/ noun

  a hope or ambition of achieving something.

- **determined**

  /dɪˈtəːmɪnd/ adjective
  having made a firm decision and being resolved not to change it.

- **perseverance**

  /pəːsɪˈvɪər(ə)ns/ noun
  persistence in doing something despite difficulty or delay in achieving success.

- **accordance**
  /əˈkɔːd(ə)ns/ noun
  conformity or agreement.
- **unremitting**
  /ʌnrɪˈmɪtɪŋ/ adjective
  never relaxing or slackening; incessant.
- **envision**
  /ɛnˈvɪʒ(ə)n/ verb
  imagine as a future possibility; visualize.
- **depiction**
  /dɪˈpɪkʃn/ noun

the action of depicting something, especially in a work of art.

- **curiosity**

    /kjʊərɪˈɒsɪti/ noun

    a strong desire to know or learn something.

- **dominance**

    /ˈdɒmɪnəns/ noun

    power and influence over others.

- **illusion**

    /ɪˈluːʒ(ə)n/ noun

    an instance of a wrong or misinterpreted perception of a experience.

- **counterfeit**

    /ˈkaʊntəfɪt, ˈkaʊntəfiːt/ adjective

    made in exact imitation of something valuable with the intention to deceive or defraud.

- **malady**

    /ˈmalədi/ noun

    LITERARY

    a disease or ailment.

- **notion**

    /ˈnəʊʃ(ə)n/ noun

    a conception of or belief about something.

- **scintillating**

    /ˈsɪntɪleɪtɪŋ/ adjective

    sparkling or shining brightly.

- **optimism**

    /ˈɒptɪmɪz(ə)m/ noun

    hopefulness and confidence about the future or the success of something.

- **pessimism**

    /ˈpɛsɪmɪz(ə)m/ noun

a tendency to see the worst aspect of things or believe that the worst will happen.

· **tenacity**

/tɪˈnasɪti/ noun

the quality or fact of being able to grip something firmly; grip.

· **pertinacity**

stubborn persistence

the quality or condition of being pertinacious; stubborn persistence; obstinacy.

Other Works From Author

- REVEAL YOURSELF
- DOESN'T CHANNGE
- THINGS DON'T MAKE
- DAWN YOURSLEF

Upcoming

- LIFE OF PHENOIX (POETRY)
- REALISE YOUR LIFE
- CITY OF SILENCE(NOVEL)
- SAEBNIUS LEINR

About Author

S.Chandra shekar vinayak known for his pen name **Chesh spire viel** or **C.Spire** and his works on *altior paradox* about human philosiphical life. Chesh spire was born on 16th of april 2007. At the age of 14 he wrote his first book 'Things don't make'. He is the author and writer of short self help books. He publishes books on online platforms. And he also authored many short books and series called *'yourself'*. At age of 13 He started posting his audio books on his YouTube channel 'chesh spire'. His previous book **'Reveal yourself'** is a self-help and philosophical book to make people know about their lives and their selves to aware them about things and ways in world . His upcoming book called *'Life of pheonix'* is a poetry about human's life. Study of human philosophy led him to develop his own paradox, So called the ALTIOR PARADOX, Which is a paradox that relates to human life and the reasons behind human decisions.

ॐ

INTERACT WITH AUTHOR ON:
INSTAGRAM: Chesh_spire
YOUTUBE: Chesh_spire
KINDLE: Chesh_spire
TWITTER: Chesh_spire

RIGHT OF FIRST PUBLICATION

Self published by **Spire publications**

SPID:22E1P001

First published by Notion press india and Kindle direct publishing

SPIRE SELF PUBLISHED

NOTES

DATE-

• 73 •

DAY-

About You